Endorsements

"Nancy has an exceptional gift of converting the feelings in her heart into words that flow right into her writing. She has a deep devotion to God and is highly convicted to carry that into her family, friends and community. I strongly believe that her book will touch us all in the most positive way as she continues to carry inspiring words to us all."
—Captain John Faist, Civil Engineer Corps.
United States Navy, Retired/Seattle

"Here are the words of a trusted guide. As a committed laywoman who is seeking to bring her whole life and self to her relationship with God, Nancy brings the much needed perspective of one who is not a 'paid professional Christian' but rather of one who sees with the eyes of a heart longing for God. Here is a view not only from the pew, but also from a woman, a lover of language, a deep listener to God and others, one who can name the intersection between my unfolding story and that of God with us. There is a gentle fearlessness in her words and relationship with God that empowers others in their journey."
—The Reverend Lawrence W. Farris is a Presbyterian pastor, spiritual director, teacher, and writer who is currently serving as Interim Pastor of the First Presbyterian Church of Ann Arbor, Michigan. Larry is a graduate of the University of Michigan and Princeton Theological Seminary.

"Nancy has a way of taking a challenging text or a difficult concept and translating into everyday language that helps us find an inspirational nugget. She is a truly gifted writer for those living with the everyday joys and challenges of life!"
—Lisa Batten, Director Wesley Foundation of Kalamazoo A United Methodist Campus Ministry serving Western Michigan University.

"This book translates scripture into biblical principles we can apply to our daily lives. It is a wonderful reminder of how to navigate the world with a spirit of kindness." —Elsa L. Byler, MA, LMFT. LPC, NCC

"Nancy Boyd invites the reader to join her on her spiritual journey. A journey that, like life itself, is more important than the destination. Although her spiritual journey is biblically based, her book contains lessons for everyone – seekers, doubters, fervent believers. Nancy shares her thoughts about issues all face who consciously seek to live a life that is just and righteous. Each chapter ends with quotes of others for the reader to continue their reflection. This is a book that will be dipped into and thought about, and dipped into and thought about again and again throughout the year, whether the year is the church year or the year of seasons. The author reveals herself in her writing and she makes a warm, loving companion with whom to travel."
—Rebecca Black, Retired Therapist and spiritual seeker

"Breathe deeply and find your quiet center. Nancy Boyd's "Journey" beckons us into dialogue with scripture and the Spirit. May her gentle lead inspire us into more deeply meaningful meditation and action. May her healing voice empower us all to claim our ministries."
—Rev. Alice Fleming Townley, United Methodist Ordained Elder

"Nancy Boyd has written a work that encourages us to take an inward journey to discover the embodiment of Christ within ourselves and our neighbors, while calling all of us to be a part of God's work in the world."
—Jeremi Ann Colvin/M.Div., Boston, Massachusetts

Journey

Discovering faith beyond the four walls of the church

nancy a. boyd

Embrace the Journey
Nancy A. Boyd 2010

Journey

ISBN: 978-0-9787472-9-9
Printed in the United States of America
©2010 by Nancy A. Boyd
All rights reserved

Library of Congress Cataloging-in-Publication Data

Bible references are from The New Oxford Annotated Bible, NRSV,
unless otherwise referenced.

Cover and interior design by Isaac Publishing, Inc.

IPI
Isaac Publishing, Inc.
P.O. 342
Three Rivers, MI 49093
www.isaacpublishing.com

No part of this book may be reproduced or transmitted in any form or by any means, electronic or mechanical—including photocopying, recording, or by any information storage and retrieval system—without permission in writing from the publisher, except as provided by United States of America copyright law.

Please direct your inquiries to admin@isaacpublishing.com

Journey

Discovering faith beyond the four walls of the church

nancy a. boyd

Isaac Publishing, Inc.
PO Box 342
Three Rivers, MI 49093
1.888.273.4JOY
www.isaacpublishing.com

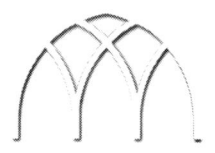

Dedication

This book is dedicated to all whose support and encouragement have brought this work of faith to reality...you know who you are. And, last but not least, to the wonderful person whose name I was given as my journey of life began, Nancy Ann Blystone- Ensley. For you, Nancy, my name as author appears in lower case letters.

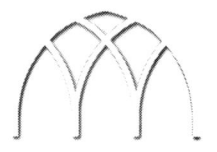

Preface

As this journey of writing began it was with the hope that one day these words would become a collection of essays and articles that would inspire others in their faith journeys. My journey into writing was begun with the humblest of hearts as I realized that often one might begin with the fear that nothing I might be able to say could possibly impact the lives of others. This may be especially true of anyone who attempts to write of spiritual matters. I do not attempt, nor profess, to be speaking for God as I see this as impossible for anyone who is not the chosen one, the Messiah. However, I attempt to share with you those things which have come to me by way of inspiration along the path of my own faith journey. Only insights inspired by God himself will take root in your life, I am merely a vessel he has chosen to share these thoughts on faith.

It is my hope that in these pages you might find a light for your spiritual path or an insight that might help you in some way to continue this journey of life which can so often leave us too weak to find insight of our own. Often God's children, all people everywhere, are left questioning why they should embrace any form of organized religion as it is clearly evident that there is little organization within the church that can be witnessed. All too often the church resembles "dysfunction" and so I like to compare that to the dysfunction within the human family…we know it exists and it is our job to work within the dysfunction to bring wholeness. For those whom this is impossible, it is my prayer that you will remember that faith is within you, within your reach, despite the exclusions you may have felt from the organized practice of faith. As people attempt to speak "for" God, lives are often destroyed and left in ruin by the narrow-mindedness we find in others who profess to represent the church. It is within you to embrace that which God intended for you to claim as your own. You do not walk this road alone, with or without the practice of organized religion; you were created by and are loved by God. If you have felt rejection it has not been the rejection of God, none are worthy but all are the recipients of God's love and grace. God is the only true judge and his judgment is seen through the eyes of his deep, abiding love.

I pray that somehow the reading of these pages will find you in an even deeper relationship with the One who brings life to our living, hope to our journey and, the ultimate peace which surpasses all of our understanding.

Peace be with you,
nancy ann

Advent Memories that Live On...

In recent months I have given much thought as to how we, as churches and parishioners, venture into attempting to prepare the most "effective" methods by which to communicate the stories of Christ. It seems that much thought has been given to the ways in which we might attempt to make these stories a little more sensational than before. Each year we hear of new "productions" done in an attempt to "top" any performance done in our communities in prior years. Having been brought up Methodist and being a familiar participant in and audience for the annual Sunday School Christmas Pageant, I am quite knowledgeable as to how these things come to fruition. In our modern society, Christmas pageants have taken on a whole new dynamic. But for most of us, our recollection of such pageants includes some pretty meager costumes and props. I will never forget the year my middle son was chosen to be a king. A KING! Anyone who knew him knew that he was indeed created for this role. In years to come I witnessed my infant "granddaughter" portray the Christ child. My, how times have changed! But, when you are the only infant available what choice is there besides the well used doll that looks anything but fresh and new, let alone "holy". What matters most is that we as children were given the awesome responsibility of portraying someone or something so important to humanity. Embarrassed or not, those memories have meaning in our own lives as well as the hearts of those who brought us to church and helped us to know that this was the story among stories. This was the story of the greatest joy known to man. An innocent baby comes to change the world and bring hope to a people lost in despair. We may have been too young to understand much of despair when we were the participants in such pageants if we were fortunate but one day, when all seems lost, we might remember what we once learned as children as we were given the roles of the most "holy" participants of this blessed event. Back then we assumed those roles believing that we were indeed qualified for a task of such great importance.

In this modern age, we see the continuing, unending processes of what are today the newest, most modern ideas, deleted and all but forgotten by the next holiday pageant. We struggle to keep up, which in itself becomes a major task (one of those Holiday stresses we seek to eliminate).

I am left to wonder how it is that we might come to believe we can improve upon the two thousand year old story of Christ's birth. What can we possibly add to that simple, yet profound event which changed the lives of mankind forever? The "staging" of a simple manger in a humble surrounding, a young frightened mother, a "father" whom God had chosen to be the earthly father of his only child, and the common beasts who shared this accommodation with the holy family. The wise men have in fact been the most adorned, by human standards, of all. They brought forth expensive gifts with which they might worship and welcome the Christ child. But even the extravagance of these men and their gifts could not overshadow the magnitude of this blessed event. Nothing in their "riches" could compare with the greatest gift ever given to mankind. Even they most likely realized this truth upon their first sight of this tiny but magnificent child.

> The truth is that the more we attempt to "sensationalize" Christ, the more we find ourselves and our productions outdated by this time next year.

Today, in the twenty first century, we are told of a portrayal of Christ's birth being "performed" in a large church community in the South. The "production" which is reported to be of a Broadway caliber, carries a price tag of $1.3 million dollars. Though 20 percent of the audience will be given free tickets, the remainder of the ten thousand which the facility will accommodate will pay anywhere from $15 to $35 for seating in this audience/sanctuary. I ponder whether Jesus himself would find cause to repeat the events surrounding the story of the "moneychangers" found in the Gospel?

The truth is that the more we attempt to "sensationalize" Christ, the more we find ourselves and our productions outdated by this time next year. It is only in the keeping of "tradition" that we can ever hope to convey the true message of Christmas to those who wander and wait to grasp the magnitude of this blessed, godly event in history.

My hope is that sons who portray kings and granddaughters who play the Christ child will find their way into our hearts as we seek to find the true meaning of the events of two thousand years ago.

As you search for truth in this blessed season we call Advent, may you find the simple truth to be profound enough to change your existence into extravagance of an unearthly nature!

Peace be with you on this extravagant journey…Nancy Ann

Thoughts for Reflection…
ADVENT THOUGHTS

"The necessary condition for the fulfillment of Advent is the renunciation of the presumptuous attitudes and alluring dreams in which and by means of which we always build ourselves imaginary worlds."

—Alfred Delp, *The Shaking Reality of Advent/taken from "Watch for the Light"*

"Understanding this world in the light of Advent means to endure in faith, waiting for the fertility of the silent earth, the abundance of the coming harvest." —Alfred Delp, *The Shaking Reality of Advent/taken from "Watch for the Light"*

"If decisive and liberating Good is to be born on this earth, it must, like Mary, find room in humble surrender."

—Philip Britts *"Yielding to God"/taken from "Watch for the Light"*

"The sign of love is the sign of weakness: a baby wrapped in swaddling clothes and lying in a manger. That is the glory of God, the peace of the world, and the good will of all men."

—Henri J.M. Nouwen (edited by Michael Ford) *"The Dance of Life"*

New beginnings: January thoughts

In Isaiah 43:19 we read;" I am about to do a new thing; now it springs forth, do you not perceive it?" (NRSV)

We typically think of January and the new year as a time for beginning again, for making all things new, an opportunity to set things straight, to "get it right" this time.

St. Ignatius wrote: "There are very few people who realize what God would make of them if they abandoned themselves into his hands, and let themselves be formed by his grace." He goes on to say, "I ask for the grace to trust myself totally to God's love."

> All too often we are quick to believe that if we are not involved in "holy activity" we are not doing the will of God.

As we embrace this trust which will lead us by our faith, we may ask ourselves what trust looks like. Perhaps instead of leaping forward into a barrage of "yes's" we may stop to consider that God may be calling us, not into action, but into reflection and discernment. Time set apart for us to "commune" with him and to wait (which is something most of us don't do very well) for his leading, His guidance. All too often we are quick to believe that if we are not involved in "holy activity" we are not doing the will of God. In this season of renewal, consider "resting" in him and "waiting" for His purposes to be born in you, in us.

Peace be with you as you embark on a journey of trust… Nancy

Thoughts for Reflection...
NEW BEGINNINGS

"I will lead the blind by a road they do not know, by paths they have not known I will guide them. I will turn the darkness before them into light, the rough places into level ground. These are the things I will do, and I will not forsake them" (Isaiah 42:16 NRSV).

"Happiness cannot be traveled to, owned, earned, won or consumed. Happiness is the spiritual experience of living every minute with love, grace and gratitude." —Dennis Waitley

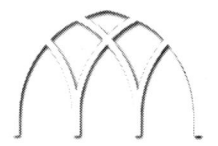

The Power of the Word…

The word began as the most basic way to communicate. Somehow, through the passing of time, it has become perhaps overly used and in this way has also become less profound or so we have come to believe.

Today, we find numerous ways to communicate and of late what is called "texting" has become the latest and greatest way to "communicate" or so we might think. It appears that communicating, at least in this faceless way, is alive and well. While this may be true on some level, it still remains impersonal and does not necessarily signify our ability to truly communicate. And, we might ask, how many words are necessary to communicate effectively? This most likely depends on whether we find it necessary to share information, such as dates and times or, words which have a deeper meaning and a more lasting effect on our lives. Recently I heard a commentary on public radio by a professor who was acknowledging the profound effect the practice of texting has on our young people. He states that he has not gone so far as to forbid texting in his classroom during lectures but is fully aware of the amount of time his students spend distracted by this practice. He states that because of the ever- present ability of people to communicate (?) instantly he recognizes the powerful effect this has on individuals. As they emerge from the classroom (if not during class time) they immediately are engaged in checking text messages because in our day and in our newfound technology there is always the possibility that there will be a message waiting for them that might affect their lives profoundly: a notice to be on guard because a gunman is loose on the campus and is threatening the lives of students and staff, a breakup

> …"texting" has become the latest and greatest way to "communicate" or so we might think.

of a relationship that has had a significant impact upon their lives, even a message of love from someone they have hoped would acknowledge them. Within seconds it is all there, waiting to tell the future of what might be in their lives or what might be ending that will impact them profoundly, a few words that might change everything.

What we may have been able to forget is the powerful effect that words have upon our lives. Only one word is necessary to build up or tear down another. It is in acknowledging this truth that we can begin to recognize, once again, the empowerment which we have at our disposal. Because we have been given "free choice" by our creator God, we have perhaps forgotten the magnitude of the responsibility we have been given in choosing our words carefully. It seems that we might have found it necessary to use more words to express our anger than those we choose to share our love. In either case, the truth remains that few words are needed to convey either emotion that would serve to build up or to tear down.

How is it when God speaks? The hearer always has the choice to tune in or out the one communicating. It seemingly is much easier to tune out God because he does not communicate in the physical, face to face encounter. God can be so much easier to ignore or at least one might think so. The "delete text" button or the disconnect button is so accessible; we might wonder, is God so easily "disconnected" from communicating with us?

> What we may have been able to forget is the powerful effect that words have upon our lives. Only one word is necessary to build up or tear down another.

In scripture many words are used to "tell the story" of God, his creation and his people since the beginning of time; in fact, the Bible is the most read and the only truly timeless text ever written and compiled. It is for this reason that within its words, we find ourselves, time and time again. But when we attempt to describe the God whom we have known, the Jesus who has been our Savior, few words are necessary. Perhaps this is why lengthy sermons often go unheard! Tell me how this Jesus has affected your life within the present-day context of our humanity. In the telling, love will always be present, grace will abound, and mercy has no end. The end of the story is always the same, is always life-giving and empowering. Is this not how our own words should be? When chosen carefully, our words can give life and empower another to believe in this love which passes all understanding. In the wrong use of words (and actions) we have the capacity to diminish another's ability to believe. How powerful we can be, for or against, the Kingdom of God. This is the gift of free choice we have been given, the double- edged sword of living a life of faith. It is in recognizing this power we possess that we must always seek to be mindful of the words we use and constantly aware of the great faith God has placed in us. It is a responsibility unlike any other and one that will indeed follow us throughout our lifetime. We will be remembered as one who empowered others and was life giving by our words (and deeds) or as one who forgot the great responsibility we had been given. It is we who will ultimately give account for those choices.

"Indeed, the word of God is living and active, sharper than any two- edged sword, piercing until it divides soul from spirit, joints from marrow; it is able to judge the thoughts and intentions of the heart. And before him no creature is hidden, but all are naked and laid bare to the eyes of the one to whom we must render an account." (Hebrews 4 12-13NRSV).

In the words of those who attempted to teach us right from wrong, "think before you act" it is equally important to be reminded to think before we speak. What we say is so much more powerful than we often recognize.

Peace be with your "time to speak and in your time to be silent" as Solomon relates to us in Ecclesiastes.

Thoughts for Reflection...
THE POWER OF THE WORD

"I swear I will not dishonor my soul with hatred, but offer myself humbly as a guardian of nature, as a messenger of wonder, as an architect of peace."

—Diane Ackerman, taken from Gratefulness.org

Trading Sacred Places…

If you were born in the fifties or before and were raised in the church, your experience was most likely, like mine, confined to one church, one familiar congregation, and one denomination. This was a part of the "loyalty" associated with the times. A man's word was his bond. Dads went out to work to support the family which on average meant two kids (preferably one boy, one girl, etc), station wagon in the garage, and, one church, forever and always. This seemed to work well in that era. I don't recall anyone ever questioning why this was so. It just worked. End of story.

As we children of this time began to leave home and start our own families, something changed. One of the freedoms we claimed was the right to explore for ourselves what worked and what didn't with regard to our faith choices. More choices became available. Mainline denominations such as Methodist, Episcopal, Presbyterian, and Lutheran became less in the forefront and newer, non-denominational ones took their place, at least in number. These newer nondenominational churches have often been or gone on to become "mega" churches, ones which accommodate so many congregants that parking attendants and security officers are commonplace on Sundays in the church parking lot. From experience I can tell you that these places are especially accommodating when one is escaping a "bad" church experience and is looking for anonymity. No need to worry, very few people may know each other well, unless one chooses to become involved in this way. For a time this worked well for me, "the great escape." This was a necessary part of my faith journey at the time. The other alternative was to escape and not return to church, then or perhaps ever. This is where many find themselves, often with good reason, or at least, good human reason. Therein lies the question we must ask ourselves. What am I to do when I have been so deeply wounded (by the church or those within it) that I am sure the only way to protect myself is to "disconnect"? This is the way in the estrangement of family members and friends. As we observe this within the family unit we are quite often left feeling saddened and wonder why it is so difficult to reach compromise which will reunite. The answers to these questions are many and widely varied and often require deep and lengthy searching on the part of the one who desires reconciliation. Often, because of the ease with which we travel and relocate in our time, reconciliation can be avoided all too easily.

Estrangement from the church has many dynamics as well. When we have been hurt, our tendency, at least at first, is to run from the source of pain. Because God has given us free choice, we are free to choose. God isn't going to show up at the door, call us (physically), or e-mail us with tempting offers to give it another try. If we remain busy enough, we won't hear him if he does try to communicate with us. Great theologians and even those in monostatic life must commit daily to focus on and receive the word God speaks to them. This does not come easily. We hear this from the most admired pilgrims of our faith, ones such as Henri Nouwen and Mother Teresa. We have been so sure that they are always "connected" to God and never struggle to stay focused. Not so.

I have come to believe that it is in the "trading of sacred places" that we remain connected to the source of life, to God through community. Many would like us to believe that our "being unfaithful" to a specific church or denomination is the same as being unfaithful to God. Somehow I can't find it in my heart to believe that God is quite this narrow minded. We are all intrigued on some level by the trading of home "spaces" as seen on TV. It often seems exciting, unless we have had to move far too many times. The trading of sacred places can be equally exciting when the "move" is orchestrated by God. Not trading home spaces might eventually find us "homeless." Not finding a new church place in which to worship might equally be so, with much longer-lasting effects. Trading "sacred places" implies that we are still in touch, still connected. Choosing to become spiritually "homeless" leaves a void which cannot truly be filled by any other "space" but its own.

Learning to trust again, or for the first time, requires us to put ourselves in a place where trust is honored and respected for all. Find a sacred place in which you can feel safe, and the messages are true for you as God has revealed "truth" to you. Know that God reveals himself to us, each of us, in many different ways. We cannot be the Holy Spirit in someone else's life and our truth will not necessarily, or likely be, uniform among all others, even those within our own communities of faith. Let God be God! We are called to love and accept his children, remembering that they too are loved unconditionally by our Heavenly Father. Remember that people who are on this journey of faith are indeed human and will disappoint us or confuse us with their behavior. The same may be said of us in light of our relationship with Christ. Is it not possible that our behavior has done the same, as Christ has witnessed our actions and reactions? We are all "wounded prophets" of sorts. Perhaps the damage done to us by a fellow congregant is truly not about that person but a reminder of a deeper, repressed wound by someone we or they trusted. "Trading Sacred Places" need not become a way of life for us. But if we are listening to God and "responding," we will know when the time has come and or the time is right. Looking for the perfect church is like looking for the perfect family. It does not exist.

When we are perfect people or perfect congregants we might expect the same of others. This will never be, prior to the great banquet prepared for us by our loving Father and brother Christ. Perhaps then we will understand fully and be able to acknowledge that our way, here on earth, was not the only way and that others too were listening and attempting to

> Perhaps the damage done to us by a fellow congregant is truly not about that person but a reminder of a deeper, repressed wound by someone we or they trusted.

respond to what God was calling them to do. Or if in the process we have become disconnected from community, maybe it won't be so difficult to admit our own shortcomings.

I encourage you to not become "spiritually homeless," and if you find yourself there, to start looking for the place in which Christ will be "present" to you in your worship. God intends us to be in "community" with all of its trials and errors. Community, as family, requires our willingness to find ways to be "present" despite disappointment. It requires great faith and great willingness to forgive and be forgiven!

May the PEACE of Christ be with you in your searching and in your finding...

Thoughts for Reflection...
TRADING SACRED PLACES

"If you concentrate on finding what is good in every situation, you will discover that your life will suddenly be filled with gratitude, a feeling that nurtures the soul." —*Rabbi Harold Kushner*

"We must not wish for the disappearance of our troubles but for the grace to transform them." —*Simone Weil*

"I refuse to be shaken from the fold. It's my God too, my Bible, my church, my faith; it chose me. But it does not make me "chosen" in a way that would exclude others." —*Kathleen Norris/Amazing Grace*

"Most importantly, I came to understand that God hadn't lost me, even if I seemed for years to have misplaced God. But this realization did not come without struggle." —*Kathleen Norris/Amazing Grace*

"The barriers which hold us back from one another in fearful individuality are the identical barriers which block the embrace of God and insulate us from the Spirit." —*Martin L. Smith/A Season for the Spirit*

The Season of Lent…

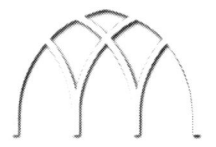

As the season of Lent approaches I must confess that I am much more comfortable with that of Advent. While Advent is also a reflective time in our faith journeys, it is most often associated with the joy of our spiritual returning to Bethlehem.

Lent reminds me of the darker side of our faith, the time when the One who came to bring peace, was himself the victim of violence. Lent is a time in our faith journey when we are asked to walk the road to Golgotha, to be reminded of the difficulty of Christ's journey and the suffering associated with his time on earth. The Prince of Peace, subjected to the most violent of circumstances never succumbed to the hatred with which he was surrounded.

> He continued to see them as His beloved even when their pettiness would undermine the mission set before them.

Those whom he chose to accompany him often disputed over which of them was the greatest and most necessary. Even they who walked with him often failed to see the truth of His message or the importance of His mission. Yet he continued to love each of them, as He does each of us. He continued to see them as His beloved even when their pettiness would undermine the mission set before them. In love, he instructed them and sought to guide them by grace. These truths of love and grace surround us yet today in our often misguided attempts to claim "our way" as that of Christ.

I am reminded in the journey into Lent of the impending sadness that accompanied the life of Christ on earth. I am called to find hope and faith in the "valley of the shadow," to know that the outcome will always be one of triumph over sadness and despair. To know that new life and hope exist beyond our circumstances and that the One who came to bring peace in the world succeeded then and still succeeds today.

Live Lent and let it live in you; be reminded of the great promise and the great sacrifice of Christ who lived among us in the flesh…

Thoughts for Reflection...
THE SEASON OF LENT

"Surrender/Submission: the laying down of the resistance to the One who loves me infinitely more than I can guess, the One who is more on my side then I am myself".
—*Martin L. Smith/"A Season for the Spirit"*

"What we are called to give up in Lent is control itself.
Truth happens to us when the coverings of illusion are stripped away and what is real emerges into the open."
—*Martin L. Smith/"A Season for the Spirit"*

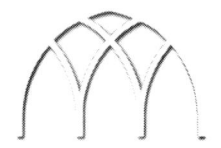

The Highs and Lows of the Spiritual Journey...
(Further thoughts on Lent)

Before Jesus is called into the wilderness to be tempted, he experiences an encounter with his cousin, John "the Baptist." Jesus finds John baptizing large numbers of people who have come for repentance and renewal, people who have come to recognize their own sinfulness and shortcomings, people who are ready to receive this new hope that is being offered. John never hesitates to inform those who have come for baptism that he is not the One who has been prophesied, not the one who will have jurisdiction over the forgiveness of their sinfulness. Of Jesus he says, "I baptize you with water; but one who is more powerful than I is coming; I am not worthy to untie the thong of his sandals. He will baptize you with the Holy Spirit and fire." (Luke 3:16NRSV).

These events have been much reported through the years; these are the familiar "facts" of the biblical story. One might ask why Jesus presented himself for Baptism, He, being the sinless one, was not in need of repentance. Why then enter into such an event as this? Perhaps we might have failed to consider that Jesus, in these acts, was solidifying his own humanity, his connectedness to us. His willingness to be partnered with those in need of forgiveness tells us much of his ministry and the purpose which lies before him. Though he is the Son of God, he is also the Son of man and desires no distinction between others and himself. Being willing to join in as equal with those being baptized, he is showing us that he has come to be one with us, not one set apart.

> Being willing to join in as equal with those being baptized, he is showing us that he has come to be one with us, not one set apart.

Though humanity is far more skeptical of following in His footsteps (because of the dangers, toils, and snares we sing of) he is a willing participant in all of our humanity, not just the "goodness" which might be found in us, often choosing to associate himself with those of low esteem and questionable reputation.

Following his baptism and the descending of the dove (Holy Spirit) upon him, Jesus is sent into the wilderness, alone, and confronted with the temptations that we might easily have fallen prey to. We might assume that Jesus, because he was the Son of God, was not truly tempted, or didn't really suffer, as we surely would have. This is far from the truth. Jesus knew hunger, loneliness, and pain just as we do. He was not exempt from the traits of humanity, including weakness. While it is true that he could have responded out of weakness to the temptation, he did not. We might ask why Jesus would not take advantage of his position and are challenged with why he was willing to endure such pain and suffering when in all reality he might well have escaped this "part" of the story. After all, he was alone in the wilderness. No witnesses to his challenges or weaknesses if he indeed acted upon them. He endured because he took seriously the challenge of becoming fully human as well as fully divine. If he sets himself apart as being able to escape these human challenges, he separates himself from us, from humanity. How much then are we willing to suffer with those who suffer? Are we allowed to ask why we need to suffer because others have sinned or made poor choices? Jesus didn't. Some people certainly suffered at the hands of evil, but some, like us, brought on their own fate. Consequences...funny how we don't like to suffer from them even when we are guilty. Somehow we hope that if we repent soon enough, the consequences might be avoided, but often they are not. It is likely that if we escape the consequences too often, we will too easily forget that we have been spared. When we are tempted to complain we might ask ourselves if we are guilty, why not suffer the consequences, and, if we are not, we might ask why Jesus was willing to suffer when he

> Jesus knew hunger, loneliness, and pain just as we do. He was not exempt from the traits of humanity, including weakness.

had no guilt, no sinfulness in Him.

Jesus came to teach us so many things, but always they involved love. Always they involved a willingness to be with those whom we deem less than desirable. Let's consider less sorting out of the nature of the sin and be willing, as Jesus, to accept our calling to be like him and to engage ourselves in the healing process of those who are considered marginal.

"Jesus, full of the Holy Spirit, returned from the Jordan and was led by the Spirit in the wilderness, where for forty days, he was tempted by the devil. He ate nothing at all during those days, and when they were over, he was famished" (Luke 4:1-3 NRSV).

"Choosing the wilderness" is what we call Lent today.

Thoughts for Reflection...
THE HIGHS AND LOWS OF THE SPIRITUAL JOURNEY

"We may forget with whom we laughed, but not with whom we shared tears." —*Tanzanian Proverb/taken from Gratefulness.org*

Speaking of Jesus' willingness to enter into baptism with the masses, Martin L. Smith puts it like this: "But instead of looking down on them from afar, secure in his own guiltlessness, Jesus plunged into the waters with them and lost himself in the crown. He threw away his innocence and separateness to take on the identity of struggling men and women who were reaching out en masse for the lifeline of forgiveness."

—*Taken from A Season for the Spirit by Martin L. Smith*
(IN A MUDDY RIVER)

A Second look at Sheep and Goats…

Today's biblical reference is to the story found in the Gospel of Matthew regarding the differences between the above named creatures of the barnyard. (It must be mentioned that the two are actually related.)

The story goes like this: "When the Son of Man comes in his glory, and all the angels with him, then he will sit on the throne of his glory. All the nations will be gathered before him, and he will separate people one from another as a shepherd separates the sheep from the goats, and he will put the sheep at his right hand and the goats at the left" (Matthew 25:31NRSV).

Jesus has distinguished one from the other based upon their willingness to care for those less fortunate: those who were hungry, naked, ill, and imprisoned. These address the most basic of human needs. Many other needs result in the area of emotional support and confront our willingness to be "one" with those in need. This we call love, the most prevalent and necessary component of a life that exemplifies that of Christ. Though scripture does not say so specifically, our knowledge of Christ and his life tells us that God truly loves both the sheep and the goats. His hope for us is surely that we will find our way to being the sheep he speaks of as caring for others unconditionally, those who are willing to be servant disciples to others without judgment. Perhaps this is what we are tempted to overlook in this story—that it is about us and our willingness to be "present" with those who are less fortunate than

> His hope for us is surely that we will find our way to being the sheep he speaks of as caring for others unconditionally, those who are willing to be servant disciples to others without judgment.

we. All too often the story is used as a means of pointing out. "who are the sheep and who are the goats?" God has not called us to love only those who are like us or to assist only those who share our point of view, which would be easy. This story is a call to love and come to the assistance of both the sheep and the goats of our society. Whether or not those we assist are in the habit of doing likewise is of no consequence with regard to our being called to be present with them. When we come to ones' assistance, it is not our place to decide who "deserves" our compassion. We are called to be "present" to all who are in need; it is not our right to judge who is deserving and who is not. Interestingly, I doubt that any of us would like to be judged before we are deemed worthy to receive assistance from God. Grace, as it were.

We are indeed called to love without exception, as Christ first loved us. By his example, we know that we receive far more than we could ever hope to attain by our own worthiness. In light of this I would suggest that we always endeavor to achieve the meeting of the needs of the sheep and the goats without ever assuming that we know which is which. If we are indeed the sheep of his flock we will live by humble grace and give food to those who are hungry, drink to those who are thirsty, shelter to those who are without, clothes to the naked, and comfort to those who are ill or in prison. And we will not be found to be negligent as stated in The Message by Eugene Peterson, "I'm telling you the solemn truth: whenever you failed to do one of these things to someone who was being overlooked or ignored, that was me—you failed to do it to me"(Matthew 25:45, in the words of Jesus).

I am left to wonder what sheep look like to "outsiders" of the local flock and if others really want to be like them. Certainly we should if they exemplify Christ and if they do, we will find the grace of God present in their lives and most often without their need to tell us just how "sheepish" they are!

Thoughts for Reflection...
A SECOND LOOK AT SHEEP & GOATS

"Oh God, your love is eternal, and we fail you seven times a day; Preserve us from measuring you by our own pettiness."
—*Peoples Companion to the Breviary/ Volume 1: copyright 1977 by the Carmelites of Indianapolis*

"How far you go in life depends on your being tender with the young, compassionate with the aged, sympathetic with the striving, and tolerant of the weak and strong. Because someday in your life you will have been all of these." —*George Washington Carver*

Unopened pathways (to the soul)…

"Happy is the one who listens to Me, watching daily at my gates, waiting beside my doors. For whoever finds me finds life…" (Proverbs 8:34-35a NRSV).

Incredible journeys…

As we ventured off to an old favorite spot for a few days apart, I went with the same prayer I usually go off with, praying that God would enlighten me in a way that might enhance my spiritual journey in an extremely meaningful way. For some reason I have always found great inspiration in this place we have traveled to. Perhaps it is being surrounded with water, which I call my soul's home that causes me to experience God in unusually profound ways. This trip was no exception.

> Today I was enlightened by the knowledge that within ME (among many other places) is the Kingdom of God.

For some time I have been dreaming a recurring dream in which I find myself in utter chaos. Since I am usually an extremely organized person, I find this quite disconcerting. The other event that occurs for me with some regularity is that I find myself reliving events and places of my childhood with quite vivid recall. I have pondered these things for quite some time and have not been able to ascertain what message might be in these events which have remained a mystery to me.

Today I was enlightened by the knowledge that within ME (among many other places) is the Kingdom of God. Therefore, the chaos may well mean that I have too many items on my everyday plate and that this kingdom knowledge had nowhere to enter in and hang its hat. "No room at the Inn so to speak." This knowledge requires me to make space and to prioritize my life in such a way that God truly does come first. This is easily said and is often believed to be true in peoples' lives but in reality I suspect that many of us, if not all of us, have a habit of putting God on the back burner while we go about what we consider to be God's plan of action for us. It is difficult to believe that God actually calls us to silence and to withdrawal from the everyday.every-day! We may recall from the words of scripture that God speaks in a still, small voice. What we may fail to recognize, or admit, is that God often loses his place in line as the stronger, more persistent voices drag us off into endless activity even if that includes a group Bible study or fellowship group. All of these things are indeed good but they cannot replace the time God encourages us to spend with him alone. God doesn't abandon us, by faith we know this is true, but can we find it within us to admit that we often abandon God, even if it is for "holy" activity?

Perhaps the vivid memories of my childhood are to remind me that God has always been present with me, through all of my choices, both good and bad. Maybe those places are vivid in my memory because I am just now coming to know that the kingdom of God in me has traveled the same places and felt the same experiences I have, because in essence, we are one. The kingdom resides within us as well as in the exterior of our experience. This "truth" personifies what it means, for me, to be a creation and child of God. It is perhaps the same as the fact that my mother and father reside somewhere in me as I am the creation of their union. Every life is both precious and sacred. How could we be anything less to God our creator and sustainer who calls us his beloved?

God continues to bless us with new knowledge of life and of the kingdom. Because the journey of our faith never ends, we can look forward to more revelations as long as there is life and breath within us. God speaks, we must listen, whenever and wherever we are, being careful to take time for the silences and still moments where God can move right in and find a place to hang the kingdom hat within.

In conclusion, my final journal entry in this time apart was: "Though the bay here is frozen, the warmth of revelation has once again become mine in this place."

May peace prevail in all your journeys into the sacred…

Thoughts for Reflection...
UNOPENED PATHWAYS TO THE SOUL

"Claiming your blessedness always leads to a deep desire to bless others." —*Henri Nouwen/ taken from Gratefulness.org*

"In the stillness of the quiet, if we listen, we can hear the whisper of the heart giving strength to weakness, courage to fear, hope to despair."
—*Howard Thurman*

The Pain of Prejudice and other such Injustices…

Let me begin by saying that I don't believe I have personally ever felt anything but acceptance in the world that surrounds me, at least in the most significant ways. My experience of prejudice has been in witnessing the exclusion of others for reasons that I cannot justify under any circumstances. I recall Jesus' words in Matthew 25:40 King James Version: "Inasmuch as ye have done it unto one of the least of these my brethren, ye have done it unto me." How is it that we come to believe that we are more significant than another? What is it we fail to see in the ministry of Christ that would cause us to feel superior to any other of God's creation, God's beloved?

> Prejudice comes in many forms, none of which I can personally embrace as the will of God.

Prejudice comes in many forms, none of which I can personally embrace as the will of God. It is in feeling a sense of entitlement or wrongful empowerment that we fail to see what Christ came to exemplify and we need only examine the scripture of the Prodigal Son to bring understanding to our potentially harmful treatment of others. It is easy to find justification in our prejudice if we view ourselves as "better than" or "more righteous than" another. The elder brother certainly" looked good on paper," having lived up to the customs of his day by being the dutiful son and staying close at hand to assist the father in his daily needs: however, what the father needs; was denied by the elder brother in the end. The father's greatest need was for his elder son to embrace and have compassion on the younger son who had "once been lost but had now been found" as in the words we sing to "Amazing Grace." Wealth, position, and power mean little if we have failed to learn the more important things—"the greater things" in life. If we "have not" compassion and do not seek justice on behalf of all God's children, we have failed in a very significant way to learn the ways of Jesus.

The road to injustice is surely crowded and has in human history always been so. We would do well to remember that God is not and cannot be bound by our human prejudices. There is no one who does not deserve the love and acceptance Christ came to show us. If we know him well, we might know that he could not find it in his heart to exclude. His only anger seemed to be in response to the injustices caused by those who embraced the "law" and thought themselves more righteous than another, those who thought they had such a handle on the rules of society (which are not always the rules of God) that they could exchange monies in the temple of God without consequence. Their righteousness caused them to feel a sense of entitlement which allowed them to "bend the rules" that might seem obvious to us. The "righteous" showed prejudice toward Jesus and his ways because they allowed themselves to believe that their way was the only way. Jesus was criticized for condoning the taking of nourishment on the Sabbath by his disciples, for healing on the holy day of Sabbath, and for showing mercy toward those they had deemed less than deserving because they had come to believe that they themselves were the religious elite, the chosen. If Jesus could be subjected to the "prejudice of the day" in his time, how much more do we exclude others by our own sense of entitlement in our day? It is possible that judgment and prejudice go hand in hand and that embracing either diminishes our ability to truly show Christ to others on our faith journey? Perhaps Jesus was telling us that "rules" and "laws" cannot supersede love and compassion. After all, love speaks louder than all the other voices spoken and heard among his people, then and now!

Know that you are his Beloved and that no one can take that away from you. Believing you are less than beloved is not the message of Christ but the message of those who have potentially lost sight of the Good News of God, in Jesus. There is no entitlement or righteousness that supersedes the love of God. In God there is no prejudice!

Thoughts for Reflection...
THE PAIN OF PREJUDICE
AND OTHER SUCH INJUSTICES

"Be kind for everyone you meet is fighting a great battle."
—*Philo of Alexandria*

"Our walls of division do not rise all the way to heaven."
—*Metropolitan Philaret of Moscow*

"Those who are lifting the world upward and onward are those who encourage more than criticize." —*Elizabeth Harrison*

Moments in time… Spring surprises

Today, because I have broken with my usual morning ritual, I am witnessing an event that would have otherwise gone unnoticed. On this March morning, which is not yet spring on the calendar, I am witnessing the falling of a spring snow. Because I am allowing myself to be "present" in these moments I am witnessing huge fresh white snowflakes falling onto the recently revealed brown grass left over from fall and winter. I realize the winter is in the process of giving way to spring, a surrender of nature. I find it in these moments so incredible that this occurs in the spiritual season of Lent, a time to surrender and release what has been to what will be, a time to truly recognize that it is a time of renewal and the birth of new insights found in the process of being willing to surrender to what will be, what must be in our lives.

> …Lent, a time to surrender and release what has been to what will be, a time to truly recognize that it is a time of renewal and the birth of new insights found in the process of being willing to surrender to what will be, what must be in our lives.

As quickly as I paused to take notice of this "giving way" of nature it has passed by and sunshine has now replaced the snowflakes falling just moments ago. These were easily moments in time I could have missed were it not for the pause in my plans. I am left to wonder how many times a day these moments of pure revelation occur without my knowing? Perhaps too many of them would diminish the profoundness in some way. Yet I am convinced that more of them would indeed speak volumes to my soul.

Though I consider myself to be a writer at heart I ponder whether events such as this can be expressed by mere words or are meant only to be absorbed into one's own soul, one of those moments where you "just had to be there." Perhaps the message here is not that you can truly "know" another's experience of this nearly spring day but that you will know that it is in the pauses of the activity of our lives that we can truly behold the magnificent!

Thoughts for Reflection...
MOMENTS IN TIME/EARLY SPRING

"In ordinary life we hardly realize that we receive a great deal more than we give, and that it is only with gratitude that life becomes rich."
—*Dietrich Bonhoeffer quote taken from Gratefulness.org*

"God is not too hard to believe in, God is too good to believe in, we being such strangers to such goodness. The love of God is to me absolutely overwhelming."
—*Rev. William Sloane Coffin/Religion and Ethics Newsweekly 08/27/04*

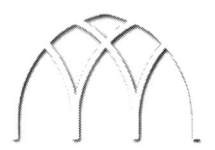

THE ROAD OF THE FAITHFUL
"WILL THEY SEE JESUS?"
(Sermon Text)

In today's text we recall the journey of two ordinary men as they encounter Christ on the road to Emmaus. Yet God has chosen not to reveal to them his identity as they journey together. As he questions them about their sadness, in his heart Jesus knows that they have lost all hope. Something they wanted and needed to believe in has been taken away. Somehow in the telling of their story to this "stranger" they begin to be reminded that what they believed in was very real; they remember the power that surrounded the one in whom they had found hope. Perhaps they dare

> We fail to recognize that an opportunity is lost each time we fail to believe…

to begin to hope that the stories they have told about the women who visited the empty tomb might be true. Yet, in their humanity, in their life experience, they continue to doubt that anything this life-changing could be true and could continue to bring them such profound hope. They remain unable, as of yet, to acknowledge the burning of hope in their hearts, so human, so like us. We so fear disappointment that we hurry to get beyond the pain. We fail to recognize that an opportunity is lost each time we fail to believe…perhaps this might be the lesson revealed on the road to Emmaus. God has chosen not to reveal Christ to them, not yet, the time has not yet come; there are lessons to be learned along the way. As they near their destination they invite the "stranger" to join them and to find rest. As the bread is broken by Christ, not in keeping with the tradition that the homeowner would customarily break the bread of his guests, their eyes are opened. Now they know what their hearts were not prepared to receive along the way. Now they can recognize the "burning" they had glimpsed along the way but dared not, in their humanity, to acknowledge. What if they were wrong? This would only add more pain to their already discouraged hearts.

On our everyday journeys, our ordinary tasks can so easily overcome our ability to live as people of faith. Henri Nouwen put it this way, "the great temptation of our lives is to deny our role as chosen people and so we allow ourselves to be trapped in the worries of our daily lives." Without the Word that keeps lifting us up as chosen people, we remain, or become, small people, stuck in the complaints that emerge from our daily struggle to survive. Without the Word that makes our hearts burn, we can't do much more than walk home, resigned to the sad fact that "there is nothing new under the sun." On our road to wherever, we are called to believe, to keep the faith alive in our hearts and in the hearts of those we will encounter along the way. We are called to remember that we have been chosen. Being chosen will require something of us, something beyond a Sunday morning spent in church. We cannot continue to expect all of our spiritual needs to be "given" to us by our messengers/our pastors, by one small amount of time spent in the pews of our sanctuaries. We have a responsibility in our faith lives. Our lack of inspiration cannot be laid solely upon someone else, anyone else. WE have a responsibility; one that God clearly calls us to be faithful to if we desire to find HOPE in our journeys and in our daily lives. There is a familiar poem of faith entitled "Letter from a Friend" in which the Lord reminds us of all the ways he attempts, each day, to gain our attention. It begins with the sunrise and ends with the sunset and all the things in between in which God has attempted to reveal himself to us. These are often the ways which we fail to recognize him because of our many distractions, because of our self- imposed agendas, and because, like the two on the road to Emmaus, we have allowed ourselves to lose hope because things didn't turn out the way we thought they would. Scripture tells us that we are to be "in this world but not of this world." Admittedly, this is a seemingly insurmountable task. This world is all we know and it is easy to get caught up in it, to believe that what is happening in our daily lives is what is most important. It is so much easier to move God on our priority lists because after all, God doesn't shout, doesn't confront us face to face (most often), and is probably the only one who is willing to wait patiently for us to fulfill what he asks of us. His voice will never rise above the audible shouts and demands of those around us. We will only find him when we discipline ourselves to become aware of his presence with us when we finally allow ourselves to recognize that it is we ourselves who must take responsibility for our spiritual journeys. As people of faith, if we are to reveal our Christ to the world, to those around us, it is we who will need to assume the greater responsibility. It is we who need to be aware of the sunrises and the sunsets that are a part of each day. We will need to recognize that there are indeed sunrises and sunsets each day, even though they may not always be visible or we may not always take notice in light of our activity. It is in realizing that each breath is God's way of saying, "I'm not finished with you yet; there is so much more to learn, so much more that can be done to accomplish my Kingdom on earth and so many ways you can use your life to show others who I am. "God might say to us," each day is my gift to you; each day has been ordained for you before it even begins. Each day I am here to encourage you, to walk beside you, even though you often fail to recognize me along the way. I do not lose sight of you nor lose sight of what is important to you. I will never lose hope in you and the hope that your life can be all that I have hoped for and prayed for in you."

We have the benefit of the scriptures, stories such as the road to Emmaus. We have the gospels to reveal Christ to us; we can learn by his example how to be like him, how to love as he loves and not as the world would teach us to love, which is conditional and often far from compassionate. It seems that Christ most often, if not always in his own ministry to the world, chose to reveal himself to those whom the world thought were unworthy. Yet, in the perfect love of God, which Christ

> As people of faith, if we are to reveal our Christ to the world, to those around us, it is we who will need to assume the greater responsibility.

came to reveal as he lived among "us," we can see that no one is beyond the hope that God has for each of us.

As we journey our daily roads in life it will be important for us to remember that God is the revealer of the unseen Christ. Our task is to prepare our hearts for the encounters God will cause to take place in our daily lives. It will not be for us to judge which encounters are of significance or which persons are placed in our lives to walk beside us, so that they might see Jesus in us. If we attempt to manage those things, our opportunities will become lost opportunities. Will our hearts "burn" when we encounter God's purposes for us or will we be so human that we will not see beyond our humanity; will we be so engrained in our own devices and purposes and so sure that we know who needs us to share our faith that we will miss the opportunity God has chosen to give us? Those in need are not always easily recognized; many have learned to live behind the masks they have created for themselves so that it won't be easy for us to pick them out of the crowd. It can be easy to assume that some have been given the role of encouraging us, of being our leaders in life or in the faith. Parents are supposed to be strong, our support system, pastors are meant to be pastors, not people in need; people in leadership positions have it all together, that's why they get the job. Consider that each of these persons are as in need of Jesus' love and compassion as we are. Parents and pastors are wounded too, are living in the same society and suffer the same woundedness as do we; their hearts need healing just like ours. It is we who must be committed to the preparing of our hearts to be the revealers of Christ along the way. Remember that Christ used few words in his ministry; his love and compassion spoke far more than any language is capable of. Our words would potentially be as the clanging cymbal if love is not present in our hearts. Love seeks first to extend the hand and the heart. It is in these gestures that Christ will be seen. The relationships that are formed in love will produce the opportunities for the sharing of Christ, with or without words. Mother Teresa, who ministered to countless num-

> Our task is to prepare our hearts for the encounters God will cause to take place in our daily lives.

bers of sick and dying, did not do so with words. By the love in her heart and the compassion she showed to those who were at death's door, she revealed the true and loving Christ who sought to minister to the needs of the people of God, all people, as did she. Hearts were healed even when human bodies were not restored to health.

There will be a time for the sharing of words; do not assume that God needs your verbal communication in order to reveal himself to others. So live your life in preparation for the encounters Christ will orchestrate, that there will be no doubt that you live grounded in and through and for the Christ who died out of an unspeakable love for us. This is the message God's people most need to know for themselves. I can use words to tell you these truths or I can so order my life that it will be evident in the living of my days that Christ is the Lord of my life, that without him I would not be capable of ever hoping to love as he loved, or to show compassion and acceptance as he did. I stand before you and confess that I have not always lived up to what I know to be true and right. What I can profess is the love of Christ which enables me to continue on every day and on every road in the hope of one day reaching his desire for my life, knowing that as I strive to live for Christ my efforts will fall on shallow ground and be meaningless if my life does not personify my "witness." My words of faith might bring more harm than good if I do not live the life I have been called by Christ to live. It matters not if I attend church each Sunday and know my scriptures well if my life does not exemplify what I profess by my words.

> There will be a time for the sharing of words; do not assume that God needs your verbal communication in order to reveal himself to others.

WE HAVE BECOME THE GREAT CLOUD OF WITNESSES SPOKEN OF IN THE BOOK OF HEBREWS. GO OUT AND LIVE AS THOUGH YOUR LIFE HAS BEEN CHOSEN AS A MEANS FOR WHICH OTHERS WILL SEE JESUS!!! AMEN

Thoughts for Reflection...
ROAD OF THE FAITHFUL, WILL THEY SEE JESUS?

"The friend of God has these three qualities; a generosity like that of the ocean, a compassion like that of the sun, a humility like that of the earth." —*Bayazid/Tadhkirat/taken from Gratefulness.org*

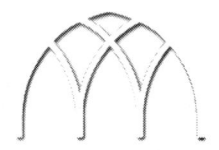

Faith and Fathers...

Today is a beautiful day filled with sunshine, a gentle breeze and the renewal of the earth which we call spring. Soon it will officially be summer. At this time of year my thoughts turn to the month in which we celebrate Father's Day. And so in light of this I ponder the meaning of each of us being the child of someone and being the beloved child of our Heavenly Father whose faithfulness is without question despite our flaws and failures.

In the Gospel of Matthew, chapter 18: 4-6 (NRSV), we read these familiar words: "Whoever becomes humble like this child is the greatest in the kingdom of heaven. Whoever welcomes one such child in my name welcomes me. If any of you put a stumbling block before one of these little ones who believe in me, if would be better for you if a great millstone were fastened around your neck and you were drowned in the depth of the sea."

> Perhaps we would be wise to open our hearts and minds to a deeper meaning that lies beneath what we would consider to be literal.

The question at hand becomes "who are the children" in this scenario. It is often our habit to literalize the words and to assume that we know with all certainty what is being put before us. Perhaps we would be wise to open our hearts and minds to a deeper meaning that lies beneath what we would consider to be literal.

As I look upon my own life journey I recognize that I will always be both the "child" of God and the "child" of my earthly father and that age does not change this "truth." As parents, even as our children reach adulthood, they remain our "children." Sometimes I see myself as the junior high student slowly making my way home from school (in Highland, Indiana), just beginning to discover that there was much about me I didn't yet understand and wanting, as most "children" of that age, to know it all and to act as if I did. Sometimes I am the less than serious Confirmation student (at Woodmar Methodist Church in Hammond, Indiana) who used this time for the purpose of socialization and not yet understanding enough about God to know that while I was busy making "social connections," he was busy planting seeds in me that would remain dormant until I "awoke" and began to seek the truth of my spirituality and faith. In these experiences God was busy tucking away what I would need somewhere down the road. These events and many like them occurred but as God would have it they did not disappear from my subconscious. The seeds that were planted would take time to come to fruition.

Many years have indeed passed since the encounters and experiences described but now, in retrospect, I see myself as a forever child of God, always in his presence, always beloved (even when perhaps unlovable) and stubborn and strong-willed as I now believe I was indeed created to be. Sometimes today I can know why I was meant to be the one so different from those who surrounded me. Today, as an adult, I use that stubborn and strong will to stand up for what I believe in, for what has been revealed to me as "truth" in my life. As a child this way of "being" may have served no purpose but its own. Interestingly, amid the strong "attributes"(?) I was taught to be respectful, kind, compassionate, and deeply caring. This much my parents were able to instill in me; when I have failed it has not been because I was not given a strong example from which to learn. The two aspects of my life have at times been in stark contrast to each other but have also perhaps been a way to help me learn the strengths of strong will for the causes that God reveals to me as necessary and important and to bring them forth with a bit more gentleness and grace.

This Fathers Day, as you review your life stories and ponder the

> Today, as an adult, I use that stubborn and strong will to stand up for what I believe in, for what has been revealed to me as "truth" in my life. As a child this way of "being" may have served no purpose but its own.

"Father's" in your life, I hope you will find time to recognize the hidden truths that you might not have considered before or perhaps not for a very long time. There can be strong contrasts between what we have known of our Heavenly Father and what we experienced with our earthly fathers, but within each circumstance there are lessons to be learned. Take time to consider what lies beneath.

The message for today in my thoughts seems to be "childlike" faith, despite age. With that comes the knowledge of my ever-present Heavenly Father and thanks for my earthly father who had to learn how to teach me to be the best person I could be, despite my stubborn and strong-willed nature. I could not be who I am today without either of them!

Thanks be to God and to my Dad!

Thoughts for Reflection...
FAITH AND FATHERS

A Dying Father's Letter to His Children by Philip S. Bernstein
"I bid you a fond farewell and ask you not to mourn my passing, but live together harmoniously respecting the memories of your loving, loyal and devoted parents."

A Covenant With Posterity by Sidney Goldstein
"We need to think of the home as the cradle into which the future is born, and the family as the nursery in which the new social order is being reared. The family is a covenant with posterity."

How To Live Meaningful Lives (in part)
"We are not only shaped by our environment, we shape it. We are not only the creatures of circumstance; we are also the creation of circumstance. "Our genes may determine whether our eyes are blue or brown, but whether we look upon each other with cold indifference or warm compassion is for us to choose."
—Sidney Greenberg, *The Wisdom of Modern Rabbis*
Blaming Circumstances (in part)

"No person succeeds in any enterprise until he takes responsibility for his choices, until he knows with unwavering certainty that he has choices, and that upon the outcome of those choices his entire destiny will depend."   —Sidney Greenberg, *The Wisdom of Modern Rabbis*

We would be wise to learn from the wisdom of our Jewish brothers and sisters.

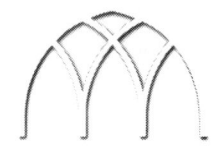

Freedom and Faith…

With the onset of July our thoughts turn to those of freedom, the freedoms we enjoy as Americans, freedom of religion and the God-given freedom to choose for ourselves everything from the most insignificant to the most profound. At first glance, freedom really does seem to be free and then we remember the cost involved in preserving and persevering in freedom, both in our lives as citizens of a given country and as individuals making choices that will ultimately affect so many more lives than just our own.

It is often said that God has given us free choice so that we might choose to love him. After all, what is love if it is forced and we have no choice but to love another? If one is forced to love another, that love has no real value; if one chooses to love another then love is genuine and a gift beyond measure.

> In reality the true reward is in knowing and receiving the love of Christ which brings with it the "prosperity" of grace and mercy.

It seems to me that often we can grow so accustomed to freedoms that they no longer appear as "gift" but rather as "givens." This thought process seems to invade our personal choices as well. Individualism Is often viewed as success. "Look what I have accomplished, look how well I have been rewarded for my wise (?) decisions in life" etc….etc…. We might even come to believe that we are successful because of what we might call the "prosperity Gospel." "God desires me to be prosperous because that is my reward for living a life of faith." In reality the true reward is in knowing and receiving the love of Christ which brings with it the "prosperity" of grace and mercy. The other choice then becomes that if God has indeed given me great financial prosperity, what will I choose to do with the wealth I have acquired? If I am indeed a follower of the Gospel of Jesus I will only be able to choose to remember the poor in whatever ways Christ leads me. I could choose to conclude that those that are poor are poor because they have not worked hard enough, saved well enough, or been wise enough to become the shrewd mangers of their own properties. What was the poor widow thinking when she gave all she had?

Of course she will go hungry, will not be able to pay her debts to society or enjoy the fruits of her labors. She was indeed "free" to choose what to do with her money but we as well are "free" to choose to demean her for those choices and so on….

In Proverbs 11:17 we find these words: "Your own soul is nourished when you are kind, but you destroy yourself when you are cruel" (New Living Translation). Every day we are free to choose over and over again in every aspect of our lives. As Scripture has told us, we are free to choose to be kind, or not. We are as well free to choose empathy rather than arrogance, love rather than hatred, generosity over greed, compassion over judgment. Consider the difference in our response when we are free to judge those living in a home they have indeed "earned" by their successes vs. living in a car which may be the only means available to them to find shelter. Consider our choice of response when confronted with a cancer patient vs. an aids patient. We might again look to Proverbs for wisdom in our choices of response… "those who love to talk will experience the consequences, for the tongue can kill or nourish life" Proverbs 18:21 NLT.

If our choice has been to follow our great redeemer Jesus Christ we must then commit to choose accordingly. When we embrace the loudest message of Christ we will indeed LOVE without regard for power, success, prosperity, position, or the judgment we are free to impose on those whom we don't understand.

As we consider the freedoms we enjoy, both of God and of Country, we may do well to remember that we are indeed "the land of the free because of the brave" whether or not we accept war as a means of peace.

We are also free as individuals to choose to live by the "power of love" vs. "the love of power" and in these choices we might either find peace or poison for the living of our days on this earth.

❦

Thoughts for Reflection...
FREEDOM AND FAITH

"We have freedom to respond as we choose, but first and foremost it is always God who acts." —Richard Foster, *Life with God*

"Forgiveness and Trust are our tools for not letting hopelessness have the last word." —The Breviary Reading/Volume 1

"God has given you the freedom to choose, the power to change, and the ability to trust." —Richard J. Foster, *Life with God*

"I believe very much that to the degree that we carry the burden of the past, which is always full of failures and frustrations, to that degree we're not free for the present moment."
—Martin Marty "On Wintry Spirituality and Napping"
excerpt from *The Life of Meaning*

"The liberator is already present and his power is already among us. We can follow him, even today making visible something of the peace, liberty and righteousness of the kingdom that he will complete. It is no longer impossible. It has become possible for us in fellowship with him." —Jurgen Moltmann, *The Disarming Child*
excerpt from "Watch for the Light"

Letter from the point of despair…

It is likely that at some point in our lives, if not on more than one occasion, we might come to experience a feeling of complete "aloneness," a point of despair from which we will find ourselves at the bottom of the pit. We may have lived and experienced many of life's richest moments but suddenly that vanishes before our very eyes and we are now looking up to where we once stood and allowed ourselves to believe that we were invincible. The following letter comes from a point of utter despair…a cry for God's love and compassion to enter in…

"There is in me this day a sadness that looms largely above me. Tears come, which do not come easily or often. The loneliness I feel deep inside which has been with me, in some ways for many years, has become more evident of late. I feel completely alone, though surrounded by many. There are times in others' need of me that I find, for a time, my own need being met. There are other times when nothing seems to dispel this loneliness within. My heart weeps because of the depth of feeling I have been given for others…it is often so lonely in this place of deep compassion. Jesus, your cross is my cross but as well, your resurrection is my resurrection, the place in which all pain ceases to be and life is restored once again. In You I will be redeemed and find solace for my seemingly incurable loneliness. I will find joy in the midst of sorrow, companionship for my deep loneliness, understanding where it seems as though no one could or would understand me. In looking to anyone but you, Lord, only disappointment ensues. There is not one but you who knows all of me, no one but you who can perceive the depth of my love and compassion for others for which I often pay a very deep price. There seems not to be anyone but you who can even really care about such things. When I am found to be all alone in this world I am able to see that when all else is gone, there is YOU and in you I find all I ever needed. You were the only one who could ever begin to perceive the depth of my need

and the truth of my inward being, which you created. The world remains a very lonely place but in you I have found my peace…"

If we are fortunate, these times of despair will not come often in our lives. For others it is a way of life from which there is no escape. As dearly as others might love us, it is often impossible for them to understand the depth from which this kind of pain is born. We know not when despair will enter into our lives but we know with all certainly from where our help will come. Only in Christ can we be fully known, understood, and accepted just as we are….
THANKS BE TO GOD!

Thoughts for Reflection…
LETTER FROM THE POINT OF DESPAIR

"The hope that is left after all your hopes are gone---that is pure HOPE, rooted in the heart."   —David Steindl-Rast, Gratefulness.org, *The Heart of Prayer*
"No one is as capable of gratitude as one who has emerged from the kingdom of night."   —Elie Wiesel/Holocaust Survivor

"You know, God's promise was never that life would be fair. God's promise was, when it's your turn to confront the unfairness of life, no matter how hard it is, you'll be able to handle it, because he'd be on your side. He will give you the strength to find your way through."
—Rabbi Harold Kushner, *Through the Valley of the Shadow* excerpt from *The Life of Meaning*

"True freedom means to be able to control and dominate our own feelings, impulses and thoughts, so that they can help us to grow into better human beings."
—Solomon S. Bernards, *The Wisdom of Modern Rabbis*

The Seasons of our Lives
Bowman Assisted Living Fellowship
Annual December/Birthday
Celebration of Life

Opening Prayer:

Lord, today we gather to observe and celebrate the lives we have been given. Though this is not the birthday recorded on the calendar for us, we chose this day to commemorate our individual lives as we celebrate the day you chose for us to begin our lives as your beloved. We give thanks for the knowledge that in all of our living you have been present with us both in joy and in sorrow for we know that we have never walked alone. In your time, Lord, the mysteries that remain in our lives will be brought to light and we will come to understand that which is yet to be revealed. Grant us patience to walk this road with you. Amen

Scripture Reading: Ecclesiastes 3:1-8

Message:

Each of our lives represent, in some way, the changing seasons within us.

At birth, we might have best recognized the Spring of our being: the newness, the hope, the lifetime of what was yet to be. So much was before us to be lived out, our own stories created year by year, event by event.

The Summer of our lives arrived all too soon for those who watched us grow. We became playful and remained innocent in so many ways. We were as yet not familiar with the ways of the world which would later challenge us. Childhood was meant to be frivolous and full of playful experience. Perhaps our years of innocence, by circumstance, were not long lived. But we grew to know that that was indeed how it was supposed to be in the early years, if we were indeed fortunate enough.

Summer left, the folly of youth all too soon only a memory. In the Autumn of our lives we began to understand that life would bring its challenges and we would have difficult choices to make along the way. In the autumn of our lives we came to understand that responsibilities would enter into our lives and we were no longer free to be at play, at will. In the autumn of our lives we too became the parents or the teachers of those who were just coming into the Spring and summer of their lives.

We would learn to be responsible in teaching them that the seasons of life bring changes and challenges. By now we had learned that children too face life-threatening illnesses, even in the spring and summer of their lives. We would need to remember the promises of God and that His plan was to prosper us and not to harm us. We now learned that this does not mean we will not be challenged along the way but that God sustains us in all that we do, throughout the "circle of life."

> It is difficult to observe this process in those we love but we have learned that each event and each journey is necessary for our "becoming" who we were meant to be.

The Winter of our lives arrives without our permission. So much of our lives have been lived. We now know how much faith, hope, and love it takes to live the seasons and allow them to teach us, in prosperity and in adversity. Now is our time to reflect, a time to learn the process psychology would call "life review." We have learned enough to recognize that those who are yet in the earlier seasons of their lives must experience the ups and downs, the joys and sorrows that we have experienced. It is difficult to observe this process in those we love but we have learned that each event and each journey is necessary for our "becoming" who we were meant to be. We want to protect those younger than us from the loss of innocence, but we know that that is as much a part of life as were the years of innocence and folly. God has held us, carried us, and nurtured us through all of our experiences and has taught us that if we but believe, we can survive and find happiness despite the sorrow and devastation along the way. This is the lesson that we, in the winter of our lives, must teach to those around us.

Let us be willing to continue to learn from the seasons we have been given, for each has taught us something of great value. Though the seasons have brought forth both challenges and joys, we can learn from each how to live out their meaning with more depth. Let the lessons teach us and those we love that which is most significant for the living of our days. Amen.

Afterthoughts…

From these beloved who are in the winter of their lives I have learned lessons that can only be taught when the wisdom of aging has taken place. In and through the lives of those who have lived many years I have found the gift of great compassion and deep love. From them I have learned much of what one needs to know in this life.

And so to my beloved friends at Bowman House, thanks for all you have given me in the time we have spent together over these past few years. I love you all!

Further Thoughts for Reflection…
THE SEASONS OF OUR LIVES

"Spring passes and one remembers one's innocence. Summer passes and one remembers one's exuberance. Autumn passes and one remembers one's reverence. Winter passes and one remembers one's perseverance."
—Yoko Ono/taken from Gratefulness.org

"It is important that we recognize these inner seasons and claim their grace, neither denying their challenge, nor being totally dependent on their comfort. It doesn't matter whether we glide, trudge, run, skip, or plod along the way. Our work is to continue to move through these four internal seasons, always willing to receive the valuable teachings they impart."

Joyce Rupp & Macrina Wiederkehr
The Circle of Life, the Heart's Journey Through the Seasons

Life is What Happens When…

In the Western world we have become so accustomed to the "planning" of our lives that it is often only when we are struck by the unimaginable that we can begin to recall that our lives are not truly our own, to plan, to orchestrate, to implement. As we make entries into our daily planners we somehow never seem to leave "space" for the Plan Bs which will enter into our lives without warning. It has been said that the quality of our lives might well depend, at least in part, to how well we are able to adapt to the inevitable Plan Bs that will become necessary as we are busy making plans.

Into my own life entered such a circumstance some years ago. It was my birthday. I had taken the day off from work and begun my day by heading to our local bookstore. It seemed as though I had just chosen the book I would dedicate part of my day to when I received a call from my husband. There had been an accident (I had already heard that traffic on one of our rural main routes had been stopped and rerouted because of it.) What I did not know, nor even conceive, was that the accident had caused the death of my husband's beloved Mother. Suddenly, the fact that it was my birthday disappeared from my memory bank, the book I had purchased was all but forgotten, and the later plans for lunch at my favorite place flew from the radar of my own mind. Time stood still…. What next, who knows how to begin in these circumstances? There were calls to be made to out-of-town siblings; there was a drive to be made an hour away in order to avoid giving this news by phone to any more siblings than necessary. At some point, which seemed a much longer period of time than in reality, we all gathered together, those who were in town. We were numb, not sure of what needed to be done next, what action we might take, let alone how we might begin to process this tragedy emotionally, collectively, and individually.

To a great degree our time was consumed by what seemed like

necessary actions. We are so much better at action in our Western world. But without words being necessary we came together to process our grief, our loss. The actions of our physical bodies did not remove the pain in our hearts or the thoughts of how life might be with Mother gone. She had lived life so fully, despite circumstances that for many might have made that pretty tough. Her final day on earth was spent on a "Mystery Trip" planned by our local banking institution for senior citizens. We never heard from her or anyone else where indeed she had spent her last full day on earth. It didn't matter much after all since we knew, without question, that she had found joy and lived life to the fullest that day as she always did. Though I often find myself struggling with St. Paul, I receive great comfort in his words found in Philippians 4;11b-12:

"I have learned to be content in whatever I have. I know what it is to have little, and I know what it is to have plenty. In any and all circumstances I have learned the secret of being well-fed and of going hungry, of having plenty and of going hungry, of having plenty and of being in need"(NRSV).

My husband's mother had lived this truth and left this legacy for those she loved. This would be a treasure for those of us who remained; those of us who needed to be reminded of the great gift of life we have been given in Christ Jesus. Her life was a testimony to what is ours if we learn to live life out of the gifts of the moments we have received, each of them, every day. She too made plans but she always left room for the Plan Bs. Her sudden loss made me realize that each of us always faces the possibility of being confronted with plans that are not our own and that as people of faith we know, after all the questions have been answered in the physical realm, that we possess a hope that cannot be given nor taken away by the world that surrounds us. The good news of Mother's life was that she lived each day to the fullest; she knew the best that life had to offer because she "took the time" and reconciled herself to finding joy despite circumstances. She would most certainly enter into heaven with that same exuberance with which she lived. She could move right in and find her place among the others with a contentment that might elude many of us as we sought to figure out how to "plan" in the context of these new surroundings.

Mother lived life to the fullest, an opportunity that awaits each of us if we so choose to spend it this way. Contentment does not depend on circumstances, as Paul himself would tell us and her life would testify. Joy is found in simply living and living simply with what we have been given, asking for nothing more than what we need or have been given. Mother's family had not asked for what we were all ultimately given in her, but our lives will be forever blessed because she was a part of them and we have been left with a legacy that will show us "a better way" to live, a way which Christ himself would ordain and Paul would witness to in his teachings.

> The good news of Mother's life was that she lived each day to the fullest; she knew the best that life had to offer because she "took the time" and reconciled herself to finding joy despite circumstances.

Psalm 139 is a great testimony to how intricately woven our lives are in God's plan; hear these words and receive the blessing that is contained within them telling you just how magnificent your creation and life are in Christ:

Psalm 139

O Lord, you have searched me and known me.
You know when I sit down and when I rise up;
You discern my thoughts from far away.
You search out my path and my lying down,
and are acquainted with all my ways.
Even before a word is on my tongue,
O Lord, you know it completely. (Vs.1-4)

For it was you who formed my inward parts;
You knit me together in my mother's womb.
I praise you for I am fearfully and wonderfully made. (Vs13-14a)

Your eyes beheld my unformed substance.
In your book were written all the days that were formed for me,
when none of them as yet existed. (vs.16)

Search me O God, and know my heart;
test me and know my thoughts.
See if there is any "offensive" (New International Version) way in me, and lead me in the way everlasting (vs. 23-24 NRSV with exception).

Our world could use more people like Mother; more people who could show us a better way to live and a way to hold on, but not too tightly, to what we hope will be in our lives. Perhaps God will be able to use those of us whose lives were touched by the example of her life and those who are like her so that we might live our days in the light of these amazing examples of the faith. Look for such people around you and remember that because they so often live in quiet joy and simple ways, they might easily be overlooked as we fill out our day planners in anticipation of what we truly have so little control over after all. Being prepared can be a valuable tool in our daily lives but learning to live out of the Plan Bs will teach us so much more!

Let the lessons of our living teach us and those we love what is most important for the living of our days.

Thoughts for Reflection...
LIFE IS WHAT HAPPENS WHEN...

"Some people have a wonderful capacity to appreciate again and again, freshly and naively, the basic good of life, with awe, pleasure, wonder, and even ecstasy."
—Abraham N. Maslow, taken from Gratefulness.org

"Our approach to gratefulness has to be big enough to embrace all the difficulties of the world." —Brother David Steindl-Rast, spoken teaching on May 5, 2007

"Becoming numb to suffering will not make us happy. The part in us that feels suffering is the same as the part that feels joy."
—Rachel Naomi Remen/ M.D., excerpt from *Kitchen Table Wisdom*

Comparative Religion 101/Life Lessons

There are always great lessons to behold in witnessing the response of those who (profess to) live by faith. We dare not judge too quickly as we might not have walked in the moccasins of those for whom tragedy strikes. In general I believe, in most cases, it is unwise to judge another under any circumstances. However, in the events spoken of herein I was left on one hand speechless and on the other hand too deeply stricken not to respond to the injustices shown in the name of faith, at least in retrospect.

It is not necessarily often that I feel my life stories behold something worth passing on outside my circle of friends and family, but God has made me witness to some pretty overwhelming life circumstances in which there are valuable lessons to be learned. We come to know this when those experiences do not disappear quickly or easily from our minds and hearts.

Some years ago at Pittsburg Children's Hospital my (stepdaughter) lay within the closed corridor of the intensive care unit. She was not alone, as was evident by the number of parents and family members who would gather in the waiting area as shifts changed and vital medical information was shared among those just arriving to provide the expert care required by "our children." Most parents were cordial but obviously overwhelmed by the circumstances in which they found themselves. Often they would take this opportunity to make phone calls to other family and friends not able to be with them. There was always the presence of a sense of numbness among us;

we could only imagine the circumstance of each parent and each child involved in these fragile moments. My heart quickly turned to the parents and family who were obviously devout in their Jewish faith. This was evident by their willingness, despite extenuating circumstances, to be faithful to their practices of eating only kosher food and doing so with regard for the other traditions required by their faith while eating. I quickly came to recognize just how much we found renewal in getting out into the streets of Pittsburg (while not able to be in the room with our daughter), in seeing life in a state which seemed so normal to us, so unlike what our lives had become like in this circumstance. What if my religion forbid me to use this as a means of "escape" (which is not even really possible)? What if I too was limited in my ability to find solace in the eating of new and varied food while experiencing the sights and sounds of the city outside the hospital where we spent most of our time? Would I have been so faithful? I would certainly hope so but then I've never had to adhere to such a rigid set of rules with regard to my religion. By witnessing the eating of their kosher food and with regard to all the other traditions of observance, I found God especially present among us. Their faith infected me and I felt the spirit of God move within me. They reminded me just how important it is to have faith and faith traditions that remind us of who we are and whose we are in any circumstance. We especially needed this in this place where we lived out the hope of our faith and its traditions. Of all the places I have ever needed to witness others' faith, this one was by far the most significant. I found comfort in their strong faith, and their willingness, under all circumstances, to be true to their God (which by the way is ours as well!) and to their beliefs. Though my faith does not require me to adhere to such stringent practices, I was uplifted by their willingness to be so faithful.

    Into these beautiful, God-filled moments enters one who obviously considers himself the "evangelist" to any whom he thought were not on his path with regard to the spiritual… His mission, despite the circumstance which had brought him there, was to set straight the obviously observant Jewish family in our midst. From there we witnessed the most profound lack of empathy, respect, and compassion I have ever been privy to and hope never to witness again in my life. I could recall the words spoken but the actions definitely spoke far louder and they were enough to substantiate my belief that God calls us to love and compassion over the need to be right and to be heard verbally. The dignity displayed by the obvious head of the Jewish household was so profoundly what I have seen in Jesus that I could only stand in awe of his ability to remain faithful even in the face of persecution. It stands to reason that a person of Jewish faith would have many more life lessons with regard to persecution than any of us would ever experience in the context of our lives or our faith. My heart remains grateful to this man of deep, devout faith who showed each of us present what it means to be faithful to your God and to what you profess. I can't bring myself to recount the words or the actions of the self-professed evangelist because yet today they bring a sense of evil so deep to my mind that I have no desire to recall them. The faith of the Jewish family was so Christ-like that it was a miracle to behold what faith can do when it is true and grounded in the God who created us. Thanks be to God for bringing these people of such deep, abiding faith into a circumstance which cried out for the necessity of such a witness. Though we have no knowledge of how their circumstance came to conclusion, we know by their witness that they will be found faithful. We were given a gift for which we can only thank God as time did not permit our paths to cross again. Their faith changed me and I remain truly grateful.

> Their faith infected me and I felt the spirit of God move within me. They reminded me just how important it is to have faith and faith traditions that remind us of who we are and whose we are in any circumstance.

Thoughts for Reflection...
LIFE LESSONS IN COMPARATIVE RELIGION...

"A spiritual person tries less to be godly than to be deeply human."
—Rev. William Sloane Coffin, Jr.

"It certainly sounds more realistic for people in darkness to dream of God's day of vengeance, finding satisfaction in the hope that at the Last Judgment all the godless enemies who oppress us here will be cast into hellfire. But what kind of blessedness is it that luxuriates in revenge and needs the groans of the damned as background to its own joy?"
—Jurgen Moltmann/German Protestant Theologian

"Our emancipation will not be complete until we are free of the fear of being Jews."
—Mordecai M. Kaplan,
excerpt from *The Wisdom of Modern Rabbis*

What Happens Next???

Despite our faith we seem to be hard-wired with a need to know what comes next. This seems so contrary to the divine within us but then as we recall Adam and Eve we recognize this futile race they and we seem to be on, needing to know and needing to be in control of our circumstances. We, like them, despite the knowledge that God can and does provide, seem to need more than we are given. If we can't have the apple then we have the need to acquire it. Eve and then Adam could not accept the fact that there was anything that was not within their reach, their ability to have and control. Perhaps what happens to them is also what happens to us, but it seems that we are not able to grasp this as truth in our lives. God did not tell us personally that we can't have the apple or anything else. We, after all, can justify our need of what we have not been given. This is where things get sticky. In our society it is easy to depict and judge what others should not be having or doing. We, after all, can convince ourselves that we would not have eaten that apple! We have the scriptures to give us the rules but too often those are used "against" rather than "for" the case for Christ. If we're not eating the apple (or been caught doing it) then we can certainly inform others that they shouldn't be doing that either. What happens when we do eat the apple? Condemnation certainly seems to come much more quickly from those around us rather than from our God who created us and loves us still. (Thus, my and many others' favorite Bible story, the Prodigal Son.) It depends on which side

> Who will love and welcome us still and who will turn away in disgust because we have received unmerited grace? (Is there any other kind?)

of the apple tree you find yourself. Who will love and welcome us still and who will turn away in disgust because we have received unmerited grace? (Is there any other kind?)

Moving on beyond the apple tree we read the words of Ecclesiastes and seemingly understand that there surely is a time for everything under heaven. A time to be born and a time to die, a time to weep and a time to laugh, a time to mourn and a time to dance, a time to "throw away" stones and a time to "gather" stones together. Yet, we will always gravitate toward the "having" and away from the "losing" side of these words. In these cases, it is so much easier to receive than to give away any of our security, our happiness, or our control over life in general. God has given us the gift of finding joy in our living and this is the side of things we like to be on. He has also given us the faith and the capacity to suffer loss and to endure. Rami Shapiro, in his book entitled "The Wisdom of Solomon" explains that Solomon (in the words of Ecclesiastes) did not so much have a negative take on life but rather that he understood the impermanence of life and our circumstances. He seemingly understood that in our need to be in control we forget that we are not and then set ourselves up for some pretty big disappointments.

Despite our circumstances it seems that (if we are wise) we have a much greater capacity for empathy for others as we age. In presuming that age brings wisdom (if we are open to it) we might begin to realize that we too have been guilty of bad choices and that those we love will do the same. Despite our attempts to live a good and "godly" life we can and will make choices that are not necessarily good for us. Only Jesus can and ever will be able to claim a sinless life. And, only Jesus, in God, will understand those choices and love us still. We would be wise to confess that we are all given the opportunity both to choose well and the opportunity to choose unwisely. We might always have a deep desire to "know" what comes next but in reality we never will. Hopefully in aging we will recognize the necessary human grace to see others through both the good and not so good choices in life. The best choice we can make would be to emulate the love of Christ through human grace.

There are so many things we can't know, we can't be in control of. The most obvious will always most likely be death. Despite medical breakthroughs, death will occur, not taking into account the age or the innocence of those it claims. Often, despite our circumstances we might find ourselves subject to anxiety and /or depression. As things escalate we could then condemn ourselves for not having enough faith, or hope. On the other side, knowing that these things can and will occur in life, we can sense the need of the other and seek to console and be empathetic to their devastating sadness, knowing that we too might one day walk this road. On the lighter side (unless you are experiencing it as we speak), we bring innocent children into the world and we are blessed to call them our own. The day will then come when they most likely will become the teenagers we have only heard about from older parents. When we cradle them in our arms, we don't need to know what will happen in years to come; we only need to know that their need of us will not go away, despite some pretty rough years. In the thick of these teenage years we will most likely ask ourselves what we could have done differently, or if we really did something wrong to cause this turbulent time in their lives and ours. Perhaps it is in this time of life, as they begin to discover their identity that they too will begin to tell themselves that they "need" to know what happens next or maybe they suffer the effects of not knowing and knowing enough to know that they don't KNOW! This might be a good time to have a chat and explain that we weren't created by God to always know what comes next and that faith (not sight) will be our guide. If we ourselves have learned this lesson we will indeed be better teachers. In the words of St. Matthew, "And can any of you by worrying add a single hour to your… life?" (Matthew6: 27 New Revised Standard Version). In reality this might be a good time to let them know, and remind ourselves, that by worrying we will only cause misery for ourselves and for others and that we might actually be shortening our lives by a whole lot more than we would like to admit.

Though it isn't easy we might best remind ourselves, daily, that we aren't supposed to know and thus we surely don't need to know either.

> …we weren't created by God to always know what comes next and that faith (not sight) will be our guide.

God always knows and is the only one who can and will ever know "what comes next." In that we can take great solace as we continue the journey of faith which will constantly attempt to teach us the way to trust the unknown.

"Lo, I am with you alway"… (Matthew 28:20b King James Version) this is all we really need to know…

❦

Thoughts for Reflection...
What Happens Next?

"Mostly we have just enough light to see the next step; what we have to do in the coming hour, or the following day. The art of living is to enjoy what we can see and not complain about what remains in the dark."   *Bread for the Journey* by Henri J.M. Nouwen

"We tend to run around trying to solve the problems of the world while anxiously avoiding confrontation with that reality wherein our problems find their deepest roots, our own selves."
Creative Ministry by Henri J.M. Nouwen

"The fruitfulness of our lives shows itself in its fullness only after we have died. We ourselves seldom see or experience our fruitfulness."
Our Greatest Gift by Henri J.M. Nouwen

"There is no certainty that my life will be any easier in the years ahead, or that my heart will be any calmer. But there is the certainty that you are waiting for me and will welcome me home when I have persevered in my long journey to your house."
A Cry for Mercy by Henri J.M. Nouwen